P9-AGI-602

Christmas Wreaths

Christmas Wreaths

TEXT AND PHOTOGRAPHS BY
Steve Sherman

THE STEPHEN GREENE PRESS
LEXINGTON, MASSACHUSETTS

Copyright © Steve Sherman, 1987
All rights reserved

First published in 1987 by The Stephen Greene Press, Inc.
Published simultaneously in Canada by Penguin Books Canada Limited
Distributed by Viking Penguin Inc., 40 West 23rd Street, New York, NY 10010.

Photographs by the author.

Wreath in front cover photo made by Gertrude Kollmann Theriault.
Wreaths in back cover photos (left and right) made by Jessica Wojtukiewicz.

Library of Congress Cataloging-in-Publication Data
Sherman, Steve
   Christmas wreaths.
   Includes index.
   1. Wreaths.   2. Christmas decorations.   I. Title.
SB449.5.W74S47   1987   745.92'6   87–8447
ISBN 0-8289-0639–4

Designed by Joyce C. Weston
Printed in the United States of America
by American Press, Inc.
Set in Windsor Light Condensed and Trump by AccuComp Typographers
Produced by Unicorn Production Services, Inc.

Except in the United States of America,
this book is sold subject to the condition
that it shall not, by way of trade or otherwise,
be lent, re-sold, hired out, or otherwise circulated
without the publisher's prior consent in any form of
binding or cover other than that in which it is
published and without a similar condition
including this condition being imposed
on the subsequent purchaser.

Acknowledgments

Thank you for sharing your expertise and interest—Barbara Bowen (once again); Mary Hibbard; Mary Ann Lopkato; Barbara Radtke; editor Rickie Harvey; and as always Julia Older.

Also: Kathy Birkebak (for wreaths on pages 83, 89, 91), Bittersweet Harvest, Box 148, West Peterborough, N.H. 03468. Gertrude Kollmann Theriault (pages 97, 99), Austrian Christmas Tree, P.O. Box 5753, Manchester, N.H. 03103. Jessica Wojtukiewicz (pages 21, 25, 31, 43, 95, 101, 106, 113, 115), The Country Shutter, Turnpike Road, New Ipswich, N.H. 03071.

Contents

Introduction

The stereotypical Christmas wreath, an ideal beauty in itself, is thought of generally as a circle of evergreen branches with a red ribbon tied on and perhaps a few pine cones attached. It's the classic wreath for the holiday season, classic because, if assembled carefully, such a wreath displays an essential elegance of color, form, and materials.

In reality, the innate beauty of wreaths also contains their potential for unlimited variations. The Christmas wreaths shown and described here are intended to convey this potential and, more important, to inspire you to try your own hand at creating something beautiful and pleasing to family and friends.

Who can ignore the possibilities for tiny hemlock cones and the big sugar pine cones, miniature toys, shiny tree ornaments, bittersweet berries, and dried roses?

And who would have thought that corn husks could be turned into a Christmas wreath? Or old wine corks? Or cranberries?

Now it's your turn.

The Symbolism of Wreaths

THE Christmas wreath shares an ancient and fascinating history with the crown. In the Christian tradition, the crown is one of the most common symbols and originates from the crowning of Christ with thorns in the mock ceremony of the Roman soldiers who hailed him as the "King of the Jews." Through the ages in Christian art, the crown was pictured often looped over the cross. This was intended to convey through these two powerful, entwined symbols that suffering (the cross) can lead to triumph and victory (the crown).

The crown as a sign of victory is borrowed from an even more ancient tradition. The early Greeks used crowns of leaves and grasses to signify victors in athletic events, rhetorical contests, and literary competitions. The most well-known crown was made of laurel leaves and placed on the heads of winners of sports events at the Pythian Games in Delphi, where the temple was dedicated to Apollo, god of the sun and creative arts. The Olympic Games in Olympia were associated with wreaths of wild olive leaves, the Isthmian Games in Corinth with pine wreaths, the Nemean Games in Nemea with parsley wreaths.

This association of wreaths with victors in a struggle of one sort or another, whether in athletics, the literary life, on the military battlefields, or in politics, was adapted by the Christians in their depiction of halos.

Beginning in the fifth century A.D., halos were represented in paintings, mosaics, and illuminated manuscripts to symbolize individuals of extraordinary merit and achievement—Christ and the Virgin Mary, the saints and martyrs. These special people achieved victories in their spiritual lives, enduring the trials of persecution and suffering. They achieved victory over sin and death. The victories were their sanctities.

In addition, the halos had a further inheritance from ancient tradition. They were signs not only of sanctity but also of power and high station. Art of ancient India and China, Greece and Rome, portrayed certain sun gods with a nimbus of light around their heads. Sometimes this nimbus was portrayed in radiating streams of light. Roman emperors in real life wore wreaths of roses and laurels, but after death and their deification they were depicted wearing wreaths radiating light. In our own time, the statue of *Liberty Enlightening the World* has a radiating nimbus around her head.

Beginning with the Egyptians

The history of wreaths begins with the beginning of civilization. Archaeologists discovered circlets of flowers and sprigs in the earliest pyramids of Egypt 2,500 years before Christ. In ancient Sumer, also 4,500 years ago, remains of wreaths made of silver beech leaves with gold pendants of willow leaves and beads of lapis lazuli were found in a religious burial grave.

Since the head is the seat of creativity, intelligence, and strength of will over the body (as well as the body politic of a nation), it is not surprising that wreaths and crowns, among the first symbols of civilization, should be traced to earliest times. Likewise, it is not surprising that the symbolism of wreaths and crowns should continue through the ages and that they should assume new meanings among the different cultures of the world.

The Chinese, for example, bestowed olive leaf wreaths on those who were successful in the literary arts. The Jewish Feast of the Tabernacle was performed during harvest time by those wearing wreaths. Arab brides wore orange blossom wreaths as signs of fertility and marriage. Greek brides and grooms, and sometimes all the guests of a wedding party, wore wreaths of quince, marjoram, or myrtle, and the custom continues today among Greeks as well as many other peoples. American brides often wear crowns of baby roses or daisies as symbols of youth, virginity, fertility, and hope.

Wreaths are found on many objects. Ancient Roman coins showed the emperors crowned with laurel leaves. Roman military generals and heroes wore wreaths of oak leaves on their uniforms, a tradition that still endures in the oak leaf insignias of modern military dress.

During the Third Crusade in the twelfth century, wreaths as a ring of twisted cloth were placed on top of a soldier's helmet. The wreath was always made with six twists, of the first two colors of the soldier's shield. This began when helmets were introduced to cover the entire face; the knights then needed individual marks or signs to distinguish them from other warriors (and thus began the tradition of heraldry).

"Corona" and "Wrethe"

The Latin origin of the word *crown* is "corona" and the Middle English origin of *wreath* is "wrethe." ("Writha" is the Anglo-Saxon origin.) The words share the same meaning, referring to something curved and twisted into a circle.

The origin of modern-day crowns of royalty stems from developments of the early-day wreaths. The Roman emperors eventually replaced the actual laurel leaves of wreaths with gold shaped into laurel leaves. In the beginning, these gold wreaths were designed as simple headdresses for rulers of nations and empires. They slowly evolved into elaborate crowns sparkling with precious stones and gold filigree, known in many countries as the Crown Jewels.

Simple or elaborate, the crowns retained their potent meaning. In 1804 Napoleon crowned himself with a wreath of gold laurel leaves, and made his point.

Symbol of Eternity

With all the variations of meanings the wreath acquired through the millennia, the oldest ascribed symbol remains today. The 4,500-year-old wreath found in King Sekemket's tomb in Egypt was laid on the king's sarcophagus. It meant that the king had won eternal life.

The meaning comes from the circular shape of a wreath, the continuous indivisible ring of life. Today funeral wreaths are placed on coffins, graves, and at the base of memorials as signs of life ultimately conquering death.

Wreaths are related to the seasons because of the endless cycle that signifies the eternal recurrence of the year. Evergreen wreaths in winter symbolize the life cycle of the Earth once again sprouting forth in spring, that winter is not the death of the year but a respite before the resurrection.

This is a reason that wreaths remain an integral part of our world culture. In fact, the symbol of the United Nations is Earth encircled by a wreath of olive leaves, the leaf of peace for the ancient world.

Meanings of peace are entirely appropriate for Christmas, and wreaths are part of this spirit. The Advent wreath, first introduced as part of the Lutheran religious ceremony, underscores the meaning of the coming of the Prince of Peace. For each of four Sundays before Christmas, a candle in a wreath is lighted as a symbol of the light to come. Sometimes Scriptures are read; sometimes children make paper stars and memorize short Scripture quotes written on both sides.

Wreaths are popular today not only because they are part of our tie with ancient tradition and ritual but also because they can be so appealing and interesting. We hang them on our front doors, as did the ancient Athenians when announcing the birth of their children, and whether we know it or not, they become joyous, cheerful, welcoming signs that link us to the specialness of Christmas and the universality of humankind.

What Makes a Christmas Wreath

THE typical Christmas wreath is made of sweet-smelling balsam evergreen branches in a circle bedecked with a big bright red ribbon tied in a bountiful bow, its two long ends draping downward. Such a wreath, a favorite of so many people for good reason, evokes the friendly warmth and good cheer of the holiday season.

The greens and reds of this simple, classic wreath have established these as the Christmas colors. The association of green and red with Christmas comes from the evergreen branches and red crab apples and berries often attached to a wreath. Symbolically, the colors refer to the evergreen victory of Christ over the red blood of his suffering.

Cones are probably the most popular addition to an evergreen wreath. Their shapes range from the tiny hemlock cones to the large sugar pine cones. Choosing the size and shape of cones depends on the overall effect you wish to make. The smallish cones create a delicate wreath, softer and quieter. The larger ones make a stronger statement, sturdy and bold.

Variations on a Theme

The essence of a wreath is in its shape, not the materials. Therefore, what makes a wreath for Christmas are materials that relate in some way, no matter how remote, to this joyful season.

The most obvious materials are those colored green and red. This means that a cloth wreath made of green and red can become a Christmas wreath. Add a ribbon, tie on a few cones, and—voilà! A Christmas wreath with a difference.

An all-cone-and-nut wreath is another popular variation. Tie on some ribbon (it can be just about any pleasing color), maybe add a sparkling Christmas tree ornament or two, and you have an unmistakable Christmas wreath.

Dried-flower wreaths easily can be designed for Christmas. Tie on tiny ornaments at the bottom or sides, and at once the wreath reflects the season.

The variations are endless. Miniature toys of any color and shape can be placed on a wreath to relate it to Christmas. In fact, a wreath you use for spring or fall can be transformed for Christmas by adding little toys, ornaments, candy canes, or fruits. A wreath made of brightly wrapped miniature packages is another possibility that may not have the familiar evergreens and red ribbon, but it certainly evokes the fun and anticipation of Christmas.

Remember, too, that Christmas wreaths can be made with artificial fruits and flowers, that not all wreaths need to be constructed of natural materials. Perhaps the most famous style of wreath is the della Robbia wreath fashioned from tiny artificial fruits and berries. These glazed terra-cotta wreaths originated with Luca della Robbia, the Florentine sculptor who lived in mid-fifteenth-century Italy. Today we carry on the tradition of wreath making with artificial fruits, blossoms, and nuts, but to display a wreath of machine-made reproductions search for the best quality items.

Where to Display

When the ancient Athenians hung wreaths on their front doors, they signaled to their friends and neighbors that a boy (an olive wreath) or a girl (a woolen fillet) had been born into the household. This tradition of hanging wreaths on front doors continues to the present, signaling the celebration of Christ's birth.

So it is entirely appropriate to hang Christmas wreaths on your front door. Not only does it relate to the central meaning of Christmas, but also it has become a sign of welcome and friendliness to people passing by or coming to visit.

The best way to exhibit a wreath for its color is to back it with a contrasting door color. Combining a light color wreath on a dark door, or a dark wreath on a light door, showcases the wreath.

The front door, of course, is the most popular place for a wreath, but not the only one. Perhaps the next favorite is above the fireplace mantel, which usually frames a wreath very nicely. Nearly any wall is as appropriate, especially if you place the wreath at eye level with ample space around it, as you would a painting. Some people like a wreath in the kitchen to enhance the already important combination of food and family.

Other people display wreaths on curbside mailboxes, under the porch light, on the garage door, even on the radiators of their cars and jeeps!

How to Store

Evergreen wreaths don't last in their original fresh state long enough to store them for the following season. On the other hand, cone-and-nut, cloth, and dried-flower wreaths can remain in first-rate condition for many years, if given minimal care. Some cone and cloth wreaths, in fact, reappear on front doors and mantels every holiday season for a generation as part of warm family Christmas rituals.

A wreath requires little attention. The main rule is to protect it from being crushed. First, wrap the wreath in plenty of tissue paper to cushion it and keep it from sliding back and forth. Then place it in a sturdy box, such as a large coat box or general purpose cardboard carton with a cover.

Label the box "Christmas Wreath" on the outside so you won't have to fumble around in your storage attic or basement trying to figure out what's inside (a year is a long time to remember the contents of boxes).

You may want to place a wreath inside a large plastic bag (the garbage-can size is big enough). This way if a part of the wreath falls off for one reason or another, the bag traps it. All you'll have to do is glue or wire the part back on, instead of making a new one. A white plastic bag is better for seeing loose parts inside.

If you store a wreath well covered on a dry shelf, nothing should happen to it until next year.

General Instructions

Detailed instructions for individual wreaths are found elsewhere in the book, but the following overall guidelines may be useful in applying wreath-making principles to whatever style you decide to make.

Probably the most valuable tip to remember is not to judge a wreath you're making until you've finished it—for an important reason: you can easily fine-tune a wreath once it is completed. In other words, if halfway through making a wreath you think that it's going to turn out lopsided or the colors aren't in the right place, be persistent. Maybe all it needs is a slight adjustment here and there after it's finished. If you stop halfway and throw it away, you could be wasting a perfectly good wreath and your time in making it.

This leads to another important reminder. Making a wreath flat on a table, as most wreathmakers do, can distort your perspective of it. To remedy this, every now and then place the wreath on a wall while you're working on it. This way you can see the wreath as it is intended—vertically, not horizontally on a worktable.

Also, when you finish a wreath and hang it up only to discover that it is somehow not as you had wished, don't panic and discard it. Simply turn the wreath left and right on the wall until it seems balanced. Nine times out of ten the symmetry will adjust to your eye. Then change the hanging hook on the wreath to the new position.

Another point is equally important. Always begin with the color of flower, herb, or branch that you want to emphasize. Then fill in around this primary color with the secondary plants. This sequence of construction keeps your focus on the primary color throughout the entire process of making the wreath.

Symmetry gives a wreath a special professional quality that stops the eye. You may not recognize the symmetry at first, but if it's not present, your interest in the wreath dissipates quickly. Also, if symmetry is too stark and noticeable, a wreath loses your interest. To construct a wreath with a subtle balance for the eye, first build the background, whether it's of balsam evergreens, straw, or silver artemisia. Then mark off an odd number of sections (three or five of them) where you'll place the main plant groupings of the wreath. A circle divided into even numbers—two or four—appears too obvious and aesthetically boring. Aim for the subtle, the interesting, the intriguing.

Here, then, are the five principles of wreath making:

- always finish making a wreath (adjust the details later)
- while making a wreath, periodically look at it on a wall to check your progress (a horizontal worktable can deceive the eye)
- when finished, shift the wreath left and right on a wall to find the most pleasing balance (the hanging hook can always be repositioned)
- always begin making a wreath with the color you wish to emphasize (after placing background/foundation plants, of course)
- always divide the wreath into an odd number of sections (this avoids a perfectly symmetrical but boring wreath)

Tools and Materials

No doubt nearly all the tools you need are already in your home. One that you might want to add, if you plan to make many wreaths, is an electric glue gun; it makes gluing less messy and more efficient. For this tool, cartridges of glue are inserted into the barrel, which heats the glue as you pull the lever and apply the tip to whatever two parts you intend to join. A glue gun can be purchased at craft stores and some hardware and home repair centers.

On the other hand, you can make wonderful wreaths with basic tools such as a wire cutter, green tape, and a bottle of ordinary household glue.

Here are tools you might find useful:

heavy-duty scissors
floral or hair spray
floral greening pins
glue
thread and needle
pencil compass
coated wire (20 or 22 gauge)
paintbrush
hooks for hanging
pliers
green florist tape
hammer
stickpins
pocketknife
screwdriver
wire cutter
fishing line
sewing machine

The materials for wreath making are divided into two general categories for the major parts of a wreath—the base and the decoration. The base can be a simple metal coat hanger shaped into a circle, or it can be ready-made double-ring mold into which cones, fumigated Spanish moss, or silver artemisia may be stuffed as a foundation for the decorations. Here are some bases to use:

> metal coat hanger
> straw ring
> metal crimped ring
> double-ring mold
> reed mats
> plywood
> cardboard
> Styrofoam ring

Decorations give a wreath its public character and tone. Just as a wall is built with hidden supporting studs and wallboard before putting on the bright public paint and artwork, so a wreath is built on a foundation before the decorations. These are the finishing items that give a wreath its pleasing artfulness.

Fortunately, the array of possible artwork on a wreath is virtually open-ended. Just as you can decorate the walls in your home innumerable ways, so, too, can you decorate your wreath. Nearly any material is feasible. The only guidelines to keep in mind are that the items should be in ratio with the size and concept of the wreath — not over- or undersized — and within a color range that you're comfortable with — not clashing chartreuses and purples. In fact, some of the fun of wreath making is matching good taste with playfulness in your selections.

Decorations might include:

> evergreen branches
> cones
> patterned cloth
> dried field grasses
> bells
> dried flowers
> ribbons
> tree ornaments
> fresh fruits
> plastic flowers
> wrapped candy
> gingerbread cookies
> bows
> seed pods
> grapevines
> toys
> whole spices
> nuts in the shell
> felt
> candles (unlighted!)
> plastic fruits
> silk flowers

As you can see, the possibilities stretch far beyond merely ribbons and cones. Unleash your imagination!

Evergreen Wreaths

THE most popular evergreen for Christmas wreaths is the balsam fir. This short-needle, compact branch is sturdy, long-lasting, and exudes a delightful woodsy fragrance, adding a dimension to a wreath not available with most other evergreens.

On the other hand, the long-needle pines give a wreath a more wispy texture. The long lines of these needles flow together for a softer appearance.

Combining a fir branch with a pine branch creates an unusual effect. Placing the fir at the top and the pine needles at the bottom where they can droop gently makes an eye-catching wreath. By adding berries or a few dried flowers at strategic spots, this one becomes a fuller rendition of the most familiar type of wreath.

However, the simplest of evergreen wreaths remains the sparsely adorned, classic Christmas version. It's also one of the easiest to make.

The tools needed are:

wire cutter (which doubles as a pruner)
spool of florist wire or clear fishing line
green florist tape (optional)
twelve-inch or larger wire ring (metal coat hanger or crimped wire ring)

The materials:

evergreen branches
red ribbon
cones (optional)

Begin by snipping the branches into five- to eight-inch long cuttings and set them aside. Most wreathmakers do not wrap the wire foundation ring with florist tape, but sometimes this helps keep the branches from slipping after you fasten them to the ring. Wrapping a metal coat hanger with tape provides friction to hold the cuttings fast; the ready-made crimped metal ring that you purchase at craft and florist shops is designed to prevent this slippage. These rings are sturdy wires that zigzag around the entire ring circumference.

Next, gather about three or four branches, place one on top of the other, lay them on the ring, and wrap the wire very tightly around the grouped bottom ends of the branches. Twist the wire to hold and cut it off the spool with the wire cutter. Place another grouping of the evergreen cuttings on the ring so that they partially overlap the previous bunch. Make sure that the wire ties of the previous bunch do not show. Secure the second cuttings, and proceed likewise completely around the ring until the metal ring no longer shows and the wreath is a consistent circle of evergreen.

As you construct the wreath, arrange the cuttings so that the center of the wreath remains open. Your aim is to end with a free, uncluttered space in the center, not a solid mass of evergreen. This means that the size of the foundation ring should be large enough to allow for the wide spread of the branches; at least a twelve-inch diameter ring is needed.

By angling the branches outward, you can build a large bushy wreath. By angling the cuttings more in the direction of the ring, you make a more compact, controlled wreath.

After the evergreens cover the entire ring, place the wreath on a wall. Step back and take a look to see if it's circular. If it's slightly off balance, prune some of the awkward twigs and branches. Do this slowly and carefully, one snip at a time before stepping back again to assess the new shape. Gradually, the wreath will conform to what you envision.

At this point, tie on some cones if you wish. Group them any way you favor—separately, in groups of three, lined up in a circle.

A large satiny red bow adds the finishing touch. Either place the ribbon at the bottom, top, or the side of the wreath. Each placement gives a different effect, so test it for eye appeal before tying it on.

For hanging the wreath on a nail or hook, fasten a loop of florist wire or clear fishing line to the back of the ring base.

This is the classic Christmas wreath —
evergreen balsam boughs and a glowing
red bow, the green and red of the season.
With fresh snow, an evergreen wreath typifies an old-fashioned Yuletide holiday com-
plete with cozy fire in the hearth.

From this basic wreath come variations
on the theme (as the rest of the examples
in this chapter illustrate). This particular
wreath is wired to a twelve-inch diameter
crimped ring. To begin, a few boughs are
bunched together at the stems and wired
there to the ring. Other bunches overlay
and hide the tied stems until the circle is
completed.

Jessica Wojtukiewicz of The Country Shutter in New Ipswich, N.H., made this charming evergreen wreath with folk art. The hearts and Welcome sign are wired to the metal base, and the delicate baby's breath blossoms are scattered strategically around the wreath. She positioned the hearts slightly off-center so that they don't look too balanced. The hearts also are appropriate for Valentine's Day in February at the tail end of winter when everyone needs cheering up. Of course, you can select any similar types of items to attach to your wreath. A cutout of your family name could be substituted for the "Welcome."

This wreath combines green and red in utter simplicity. Its appeal stems from a sort of double wreath effect, a wreath within a wreath. The red wild rose hips are first attached to a metal ring, and that in turn is wired to the evergreen wreath for the double effect.

23

The circle is the essential form of a wreath, but the decorative or interior part of it can be one of an endless number of forms. This wreath, for example, presents an active upper half with the cones angled in different directions, lending the wreath movement. At the same time, the red berries from swamp maples are interspersed throughout the wreath as a calming, unifying background. Except for the ribbon, only these two items are included, and yet the overall effect generates a feeling of more elements. The cones, in fact, are placed not helter-skelter but in a subtle grouping of three threes. This shows how a lively looking wreath can be made with minimum decorations.

All-natural wreaths represent the true tradition of the ancient symbolism of organic life in recurring cycles. On the other hand, some plastic wreaths can be attractive. This wreath is made of plastic parts to represent evergreen branches, laurel leaves, and grapes (the few natural cones are the exception). The snow is from the sky, not the store, and won't last the decades that this wreath has. Natural evergreen wreaths weather only a holiday season. Artificial wreaths last many years —an advantage, if you want to trade fresh-ness for plastic. You can assemble this kind of wreath by buying similar parts at craft shops.

This starkly elegant circle of mountain laurel offers an alternative, streamlined rendition of a more busy-looking evergreen wreath. The simple red ribbon ties it all together for the traditional green and red holiday colors. Actually, this is one of a pair of laurel wreaths on a large paneled entrance. They greet visitors and make a handsome welcome as the guests come up the front steps. If you make a similar wreath, remember that the fullness of this wreath compensates for an absence of decoration.

The color coordination of the ribbon and flowers generates the central appeal of this wreath. The eye first catches the pretty pink of the ribbon matched by the wispiness of the dyed baby's breath blossoms (the white baby's breath is natural; the purple is also dyed). Then you notice the model bird nested in Spanish moss, an imaginative touch. If you copy this example, use only commercially fumigated moss to avoid trouble with insects.

This is a delightful, playful wreath with maverick art deco colors. You might substitute a Santa Claus, reindeer, or other Christmastime ornament in cotton "snow" for the bird.

Wreathmakers sometimes deliberately shy away from holly for fear of the thorny leaves, but if you work slowly and carefully, and wear garden gloves, you'll find holly easier to work with than supposed. No matter how thorny the issue is, other wreathmakers can't resist using this typical Christmas plant.

American holly favors moist terrains and thrives in the river bottomlands of the Southeast, especially in the Great Smoky Mountains. Its thick, sturdy, spiny leaves are richly colored. The flowers appear in May and June, but on the tree the shiny berries hold throughout the winter. Combined with its bright red fruits (found only on the female tree), American holly forms a cheery, old-time wreath.

The berries on this example are grouped and spaced with a good eye for underplayed balance.

Here's a double-time wreath—a front-porch greeter both in daytime and at night. This is assembled with a good understanding of how the lights can be used to full advantage. First of all, the lights, being miniature, don't produce a glare that's conspicuous and obfuscates the wreath. These are just fragile sparks in the dark, almost like fireflies. The lights are also spaced irregularly to avoid a too-perfect symmetry.

Secondly, the red silk flowers are plentiful enough so that the lights show off their color at night. Otherwise, the wreath would be scarcely distinguishable and colorless. The background mountain laurel leaves are simple and to the point.

The porch light is turned off to give the wreath full attention. From a distance, such a nighttime wreath adds an extra warmth to any friendly front porch.

5

Cone and Nut Wreaths

THE trees we call conifers produce their seeds in cones instead of flowers. So, in effect, cones from pines, firs, hemlocks, and other conifers are the flowers of these evergreens. Attaching cones to evergreen wreaths, therefore, makes an entirely natural combination.

At the same time, wreaths made solely of cones, like those entirely of dried blossoms or laurel leaves, offer their own special appeal. An advantage of cone-and-nut wreaths is their durability. While evergreens dry out in a season, cone-and-nut wreaths can last generations in a family.

Since cones come in a wide variety of shapes and sizes, an all-cone wreath may have quite a range of textures. Combining the long, narrow, tightly shaped sugar pine cone; the rather unkempt, open eastern white pine cone; the rounded, closed, tubular Virginia and pitch pine cones; and others produces a pleasing spectrum of silhouettes and patterns.

Then, when you mix cones with nuts in the shell, the texture possibilities increase. Almonds and hazelnuts add smooth, streamlined outlines and surfaces. Walnuts, pecans, and Brazil nuts give bulk and an extended range of color.

Don't stop here. A multitextured wreath can evolve further into a complex mosaic of cones, nuts, pods, grasses, and seeds. Big lotus pods, milkweed pods, wheat stems, corncobs, and acorns (plus any similar plant and pod of nature you find) combine for a real stop-and-stare door display.

Preparing Cones and Nuts

If you collect fallen cones and nuts from the woods or orchards, swirl them in a bucket of water to remove any dirt and sand. Then lay them on a baking sheet and place them in a 200-degree-Fahrenheit oven for thirty minutes. This melts away any resin or pitch on the cones and kills any insects inside the nuts.

You can alter cones, pods, and nuts to make unusual shapes. For example, to make cone rosettes (cones that look like flower blossoms), simply take a pine cone in your hand and twist it in half (illus. 1). The bottom half of the cone will look like a wild brown daisy with flat petals (illus. 2). You can also saw the cone into sections for the same result.

Besides this, try adding a center point to the rosettes. Take an acorn and remove the outer-half covering of the rounded nut section. Then with ordinary household glue, join the acorn nut to the center of the cone rosette, creating an unusual "black-eyed Susan" effect.

The heel coverings of acorns add subtle texture to a wreath, especially

1

2

if you find them in the unbroken natural state with two nuts joined to one stem. Attach these acorn coverings to the wreath hollowside outward.

Using halves of milkweed pods is another way of giving your wreath added points of interest. Place the half pods hollowside outward, like fox ears.

Making the Wreath

You can use several different foundations for cone-and-nut wreaths, but they must be sturdy enough to support the finished weight. Large wreaths on unsupported straw rings or weak cardboard may sag. Cone wreaths are better built on a circle of plywood, pressed particleboard, or metal-ring molds.

The wreathmaker shown here is using a green-colored, double-ring wire mold; you can purchase these at craft stores (illus. 3). To make the wreath, insert the cones into the ring base. They can be wired to the ring for further security. Continue this until the circle is completed.

As shown here (illus. 4) in the upper half of the wreath, the inserted cones serve as the base for the primary decoration that will face outward.

3

4

The lower half here shows a variety of decorative cones attached to the base cones.

You can attach the decorative cones either by wiring or gluing them. An electric glue gun (illus. 5) is handy and easy to use. Wiring takes more time, and sometimes produces a more secure wreath. To use wire, slide it under the leaves and around the cone. Then twist the wire ends tight to the ring mold. Some wreathmakers wire even the thumb-size hemlock cones and nuts, sometimes drilling holes through the nuts for the wire. The method you choose depends on how carefully the finished wreath will be treated and the amount of time you wish to spend.

5

Cones come in such a wide variety of shapes and sizes that they offer wonderful potential for wreaths. This one is an example of a close-knit, evenly textured wreath. Its circumference is carefully proportioned and rounded. Notice at the edge of the circumference how the cones for the base barely show. The tight grouping of the cones and nuts creates a deceptively smooth surface.

Up close you see that this wreath is chock-full of different kinds of cones and cone rosettes, but they're placed like a carefully considered puzzle. The variety of nuts (almonds, hazelnuts, Brazil nuts, walnuts, pecans) gives the wreath not only spots of smooth textures contrasting with the cones but also a spectrum of browns.

In addition, the handsome brass door knocker becomes an integral part of what the wreath says as a greeting. It's a visual reminder of the importance of where and how to place a finished wreath.

This wreath shows how valuable small color accents are. The wreathmaker wisely refrained from attaching a ribbon. Instead, she relied on the red yarrow and white statice to brighten the browns throughout the wreath. Besides this, the contrasting textures of the predominant rough-toned cones and smooth nuts combine with the judicious use of color to create an aesthetic that sparks your interest. This interest probably wouldn't be as acute if only the reds were included, because the softer silvers make a smoother color transition from the bold reds to the somber browns.

Texture in this wreath predominates for its jubilant use of cones, lotus pods, corncobs, milkweed pods. The sense of texture, however, stems not only from the form of the cones and pods but also from how they are placed together on the wreath. The feeling of looseness imparts a heightened feeling of texture, and this in turn gives a sense of playful freedom and animation.

This wreath reminds us to keep alert for the leftover products of nature. A stroll through any nearby field and woods can reap rewards if we see fall landscape in terms of wreath making.

The handsomeness of this wreath is bolstered by the beauty of the front door. The cone part of the wreath is relatively simple, with little extended variety of shapes, which is as it should be for a background. The main feature is relatively uniform — the artificial crab apples and leaves. The apples are so plentiful and bold that this coupling of the uniformity and simplicity with the cones turns this into a most attractive wreath.

This is a large wreath, and a ribbon hung at the bottom or side would have been out of place. But the wreathmaker saw the perfect spot — at the top, so that the ribbon adds color and line within the wreath itself.

Made by Barbara Radtke of Mill Village Antiques in Francestown, N.H., this giant wreath measures thirty inches in diameter. The inner circle is twelve inches in diameter, the cone section nine inches wide. She made it fifteen years ago (cone wreaths last!) from fir and white pine cones gathered around the Ft. Collins, Colo., area. Hickory nuts, pecans, buckeyes, and Brazil nuts are scattered throughout.

She started with a base of 3/8-inch plywood cut to the above dimensions. Then she glued a base of white pine cones on the plywood and continued to add cones and nuts (she used linoleum paste for the glue). With the wreath board on a large table, she could walk around it as she worked.

Cloth Wreaths

CLOTH wreaths have several advantages over evergreen and nut wreaths. They will last for generations, can be made with any color that suits your fancy, and also are washable. And nonallergenic.

Surprisingly, for the simpler cloth wreaths, you don't need a sewing machine, nor do you have to sew by hand. Sometimes you need only a pair of scissors and a stapler to attach the cloth to a cardboard backing.

For more complicated wreaths, such as braided ones, the steps are slightly more involved.

Virtually any stuffing works for cloth wreaths, but wreathmakers find that polyester fiber, purchased in small bags at craft stores, is the most suitable. It's uniform in texture and very malleable so that the surface of your wreath doesn't bulge where it shouldn't. On the other hand, old sheets and cotton are useful, too.

Making a Braided Wreath

The following instructions refer to the finished wreath shown on page 55.

First of all, decide which material and color you wish to use. This wreathmaker selected the Christmas colors of evergreen, ribbon red, and winter white for the braids.

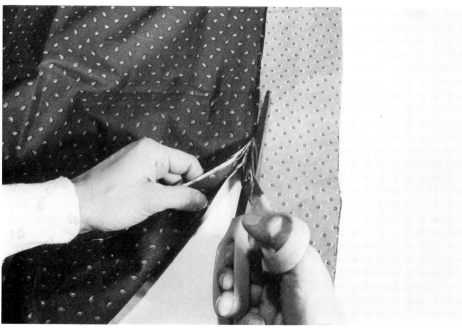

Next, measure and cut strips (illus. 6) of three pieces of each material three and a half to four inches wide and forty-five inches long (standard forty-five-inch fabric width).

Fold each strip lengthwise, right sides together, and sew with a quarter-inch seam. Turn each strip right side out to make a long hollow tube. To give support and girth to the braids, you need to stuff them with pliable, sturdy material, such as an old sheet.

To pass strips of the sheet through the braid tube, fasten a safety pin to one end of the sheet strip. Insert the pin into one end of the braid and work the pin and the sheet through the tube (illus. 7). Pull the sheet through the other end of the braid and remove the pin (illus. 8).

7

8

Now smooth the stuffing in the braid as much as possible by rolling the braid back and forth. Cut off any excess of the sheet stuffing and sew each end of the braids closed.

Lay the three stuffed braids on a worktable and braid them evenly and snugly (illus. 9).

9

10

Form a metal coat hanger into a circle (or use a crimped metal ring).

Fit the braided strips onto the ring. Then with heavy thread, sew the braids onto the metal ring (illus. 10).

Turn the wreath over and perfect the shape by hand. Once the basic wreath is finished, attach a bow or ribbon of your choice with wire or thread (illus. 11). Other items could be attached, such as miniature toys, fruits, flowers, blossoms, or candies.

11

Barbara Bowen of Hancock, N.H., shows the steps to making this colorful cloth wreath on the previous pages. The choice of green, red, and white makes this a Christmas wreath, and the finishing touch of the lace bow adds a softness in keeping with the gentleness of the braid, which is not tight.

At this stage, you could attach a minia-ture toy, a candy cane, or something simi-lar. Probably the best place to hang it would be at the top inside of the wreath so that the toy would hang framed inside the circle.

With three equally important colors in the wreath, the color of the door in the background should highlight the wreath, not clash with one of the colors. This dark blue door shows off the special simplicity of this winning wreath.

This is an example of how speed in design-ing a wreath is belied by the choice and placement of the decoration. The backing for this is simply sturdy cardboard cut to size. Then cut material is tucked tight around polyester filler (to give the wreath dimension and bulk) and stapled to the cardboard.

Next, a joyful string of bells is placed off-center and sewn onto the wreath. The ribbon then is attached directly opposite the bells to give balance on a diagonal. Placing decorations slightly off-center or on the diagonal is effective when you analyze this wreath. Think how bland and predict-able this one would be if the bells and rib-bon were placed exactly top and bottom, or left and right. Remember that off-center isn't off-kilter, just on target.

The snowflakiness of the lace on this wreath suggests the winter season, the green felt the evergreens that last no matter what. This, too, is built on a cardboard cutout base. First, polyester fill is wrapped and secured with green felt, then stapled to the cardboard. Next, the lace is wrapped and secured around the felt loop, revealing the green through the lace.

The fringe felt is stapled to the base also, and could have been the end of the wreath making. Stopping at this stage would have resulted in too plain a wreath. The wreathmaker instead envisioned the detail that ties the parts together—she glued cut "snowflakes" from leftover lace used for the center loop, an uncomplicated but creative inspiration. It's an example of how to use small parts of a large section to integrate the whole.

Grapevine Wreaths

GRAPEVINE wreaths put striking texture and line on your front door. They're relatively easy to make, and they form a base for many decorative possibilities.

Late fall is the best time to harvest grapevines, when their leaves and grapes have fallen off. The vines are plentiful in this country, and none is poisonous. You'll most likely see the vines climbing tree trunks along streams and other water sources. They form a tangle of brown, Tarzan-like ropes. Wear gloves to pull the vines down, and use pruning shears to cut them free.

The vines will be rather stiff and springy. The day you make the wreaths, it's a good idea to soak the vines in water for a couple hours or so to make them more pliant. This isn't absolutely necessary, but it certainly helps. A filled bathtub or large workroom tub does the job.

You may want to spray paint a grapevine wreath like the one shown later in this section. Some sprays today have gold glitter in white paint for an elaborate effect.

Making Grapevine Wreaths

After soaking the vines, decide whether you wish to keep on the tendrils, the small offshoots that curl into fanciful twists and turns (illus. 12). They can give a wreath added interest; without them, the wreath presents a cleaner and simpler frame.

Next, take a short strip of vine and form it into a circle by hooking one end under the vine so that it holds by its own pressure (illus. 13). Continue weaving strips in and out of this circle until you have the thickness you want (illus. 14). You can tie the vines together, but this usually isn't necessary. Also, it's easy to hang a grapevine wreath on a hook by one of its own vines.

12

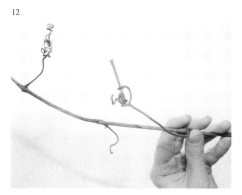

13

14

Some wreathmakers use makeshift molds to keep the circle of the wreath as uniform as possible. An overturned bucket or pail to wrap the vines around as you construct it is one method. Some use the rotor inside a washing machine!

Once the basic form is finished, add whatever decorations you wish. Orange-colored bittersweet berries make an appealing combination (illus. 15). Simply insert bittersweet twigs into the grapevine at various intervals.

15

16

Or wire a bouquet of dried flowers to the wreath (illus. 16). Candy canes and a red ribbon change grapevine wreaths into Christmas wreaths. Miniature toys, wrapped candies, Christmas tree ornaments, red silk flowers provide other Yuletide accents.

The elementary attractiveness of this grapevine wreath is broadened by its form and bulk. The wreathmaker took her cue from the tangle of the vines in their natural state and wove this wreath with some of this freedom. Making the wreath thick and bold snares our attention. Then when the branches and berries of bittersweet are added, the bright beadwork announces the staying power of midwinter nature.

As already mentioned, grapevines are best harvested in fall when the leaves are gone. It's advisable to soak the vines in a tub of water for a couple hours in order to twist them easily into the wreath shape, especially for a wreath with cleaner lines, as in the next example.

This shows how grapevines can have compact, clean lines if first soaked and circled with precision. The plaid ribbon wrapped around the vines unifies the wreath. Actually, this wreath is more complicated and symbolic of Christmas than may first appear. The holly and berries, of course, are typically Christmas, the baby's breath gives a hint of winter, and the toy hunting horn signifies the musical joy that accompanies the holidays.

Spray painting grapevines after they're formed into a wreath creates a festive look. This wreath is formed broad and flat. The bluish penny-shaped eucalyptus leaves are angled in a graceful sweep upward as if holding the grapevines. The reds of the ribbon, berries, and candle are triangled beautifully and give the wreath a jubilant, airy tone.

When you spray paint such a wreath, lay it on newspapers and be sure to spray it heavily and on all sides. Cover all areas so that, just as crimped-ring molds on evergreen wreaths shouldn't show, no unpainted brown spots are visible. The attention to details makes wreaths especially attractive. Don't light the candle!

Gift Box Wreaths

B RIGHTLY wrapped gifts are an integral part of Christmas, so nothing could be more natural than to make a wreath of gift boxes in miniature.

Some wreathmakers attach a few miniature boxes on evergreen wreaths, while others make wreaths entirely of wrapped boxes. The wreath on page 75 shows an alternative design of gift boxes mixed among silk flowers and leaves, plus miniature toys scattered around for surprise.

The steps for gift box wreaths are somewhat detailed and time-consuming, but the end result will last for many enjoyable years. Here are the basic steps:

First, draw a wreath shape on a substantial piece of paperboard about fourteen inches in diameter and with a five-inch center hole. Then with a razor blade or heavy-duty scissors, cut out the shape (illus. 17).

Next, cover the paperboard base with colored tissue paper (illus. 18). This way, if any of the base shows behind the boxes and ornaments, an appropriate color will show, not the paperboard. Green or red tissue paper is the best to use for a Christmas wreath. Fit the paper around the paperboard and tape securely.

To make the miniature gift boxes, dismantle a corrugated cardboard box. Then cut strips of the cardboard across the corrugation in varying

17

18

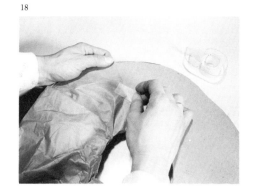

lengths (illus. 19). The sizes can range from three inches long by one inch wide to six inches by three inches.

Now bend the cardboard strips to form little boxes. Two sides will remain open. Tape the joints together so that the boxes hold their shape (illus. 20). Part of the charm of such a wreath is the variety of the sizes of boxes.

To give the boxes internal support and to close off the two open ends,

19

20

21

22

prepare strips of newspaper. Stuff these strips into the boxes just enough to fill them (illus. 21). Make sure the newspaper forms the "sides" of the two open ends but is not sticking out beyond the edges of the rest of the box. Tape over the newspaper ends to secure.

Now that your miniature boxes are ready, wrap them with ordinary holiday gift paper (illus. 22). Using wrapping paper with a variety of scenes, colors, and brightness adds to the interest in a wreath, just as with actual

23

24

presents under a Christmas tree. Add some gold, red, silver, and green foil.

The flowers and leaves can be stapled or glued to the wrapped paperboard base (illus. 23).

After the flowers are in place, glue the gift boxes to the wreath (illus. 24). Group them in different sizes and try to cover as much of the wreath base as possible.

The final touch is to glue any miniature toys, figurines, acorns, candy, or ornaments anywhere you wish. The more detail the better.

Add a loop of thread or fishing line to the back of the base and your gift box wreath is ready to dazzle.

This playful gift box wreath is the end result of the steps outlined on the previous pages. The sense of miniature has natural, special appeal for us, and this engaging wreath confirms it. Notice how the sizes of the gifts vary, and also the toys — the hobbyhorse glued to one present, teddy bears and harps placed in semisecret spots. The more detail, the better. It keeps the viewer searching for surprises.

Green paper is wrapped around the paperboard base so that if any of the base shows it will blend in with the stems and leaves. Notice, too, how the red silk blossoms form a triangle but are set very slightly off-center to give a pleasing harmony. Remember that an odd number of divisions in wreaths is more kindly to the eye.

In gift box wreaths, lots of carefully placed details feed the viewer's imagination and enjoyment. This wreath, made by Eleanor Higgins of Phoenix, Ariz., received so much comment in the companion book **Wreaths for All Seasons** *that it calls for a repeat performance here. Of course, this wreath typifies to the nth degree the Christmas spirit of gift-giving and brings smiles and anticipation to all who see it—particularly children.*

The wreath is built on cutout cardboard. Every inch is covered with gift boxes, and miniature toy animals and playthings are interspersed among the boxes. If you make a similar wreath, one hint for success is to imitate the various sizes of the boxes and to wrap them in a broad range of shiny paper, just as those you would see under a Christmas tree.

Dried-Flower, Spice,
Fruit—and Cork!—Wreaths

DRIED-FLOWER wreaths have the advantage of providing summer color in the deep winter of the Christmas holidays. In addition, wreaths made of certain plants such as santolina or sage exude long-lasting fragrances that linger in your kitchen, living room, and bedroom.

Dried-flower wreaths can be transformed for Noel by small touches. Attach a few Christmas tree balls, cones, laurel leaves, or red ribbons, and the festivity appears.

Try building wreaths with some art deco colors, such as mauve, purple, and violet pink. They put a touch of glamorous sophistication into your holidays.

How To Dry Flowers

Nearly any kinds of blossoms, stems, and leaves may be dried. You can purchase dried flowers at craft and florist shops, but drying them yourself sees you through the entire process of this kind of wreath making, especially if you harvest the flowers from your own garden.

To dry the flowers of your choice, place them in a dry room for about two to four weeks, depending on the moisture in the plants and your locale, house, and season of the year. Wreathmakers hang the plants upside down—blossom end downward. This helps prevent the blossoms from breaking off, which they are likely to do if placed upright as they dry out and droop over.

One way of drying plants is to set up a series of wooden or metal poles in a room. Then tie bunches of the plants upside down and hang them on the bottom rung of metal clothes hangers. Hook the hangers over the poles and leave the plants until dried.

Another method is to speed up the process with silica gel. This is a desiccant, a grainy substance that absorbs the moisture of the blossoms and stems. It can be purchased at craft stores and some home repair centers. Silica gel is good to use for the more delicate blossoms, such as baby's breath. Mixing it half and half with cornmeal extends the supply of the silica gel, which can be used indefinitely with other plants. Simply place a layer of silica gel in a shallow box or baking sheet. Lay the plants on the gel. Then cover the plants with more silica gel. Drying plants this way takes about five or six days.

Background and Decorative Plants to Use

The bases for dried-flower wreaths can be crimped rings, multiwire double-ring molds, flat-woven hemp mats, straw or Styrofoam rings. These are the solid structures to which you attach your background plants. For example, the popular silver king artemisia is a pliable, spindly, greyish plant excellent as a background color that gives both fullness and texture to your finished wreath; it makes a neutral backdrop on which to highlight your decorative colors.

Other useful background plants include fumigated Spanish moss, lemon balm, santolina, tarragon, southernwood.

For the predominant colors and shapes of the wreath, choose your favorite flower and stem. Nearly any combination that you envision as harmonious and interesting is perfectly all right. Pods, seeds, berries, burs—these, too, help make an intriguing wreath.

Some decorative plants include yarrow (Coronation Gold), baby's breath, statice, asters, Chinese lantern, goldenrod, parsley, ruscus, sweet basil, sage, oregano, cinnamon sticks, star anise, nutmeg.

Making a Dried-Flower Wreath

If you use a straw ring or woven hemp base, florist pins or large U-shaped greening pins are best to secure the plants in place. For a multiwire double-ring mold, place your background plant, such as silver king or queen artemisia, inside the wire bed.

The decorative part of the wreath includes the colors and shapes you want to emphasize. Use green florist tape to gather and hold groups of plant stems securely. Work gently with dried flowers and herbs; they tend to break easily. Try to keep the bunches the same size to give the finished wreath a pleasing symmetry.

Wire some of the less delicate plants together at the stem base. Green-coated florist spool wire or craft thread blend into the background. This is one of the aims of wreath making—to design and construct a wreath

25

26

so that the base mold, thread, wire, tape, and pins don't show.

Once the plant stems are wired or taped together in bunches, it's time to attach them to the wreath. For straw or Styrofoam bases, pins work well. For hemp bases, gluing is recommended. Either gluing, wiring, or taping plants to a crimped ring or double-ring mold does the job.

To make the crownlike wreath illustrated here, a crimped ring is used for the base support (illus. 25). Five plants decorate the wreath—dried red roses, dusty miller, German statice, peppergrass, hemlock cones, and eucalyptus leaves.

The stems of the plants are taped together and then taped to the crimped ring (illus. 26). The same sequence of plants continues around the ring until completed. The tiny hemlock cones, for example, are glued by the electric glue gun (illus. 27). Since this wreath is narrow and delicate, it needs no loop for a hook. Simply hang it on a nail in a door.

27

This crownlike wreath, made by Kathy Birkebak of Bittersweet Harvest in West Peterborough, N.H., evokes an uncommon, serene beauty. The blending of textures and colors comes from an expert. The simplicity of the effect can deceive you because there's more here than meets the eye.

The wreath is built on a crimped ring. The bluish eucalyptus leaves and dried red Gabrielle roses reign as colors, but dusty miller, German statice, and peppergrass mute the dominance. Tiny hemlock cones give the wreath a wintry tone.

This is a good example of a small-scale wreath that delivers a refined message of Christmas. When a crownlike wreath is hung at a strategic point on a door, the symbolism is ancient and profound—the victorious crown wrapped around the cross of suffering.

Dried-flower wreaths change the pace for those wishing to deviate from the popular evergreen and cone display. This example shows how a minimum but appropriate number of decorations transforms a year-round wreath to a Christmas wreath. The animating swirl of silver artemisia forms the essential wreath, but when a few tiny tree ornaments are added, right away the wreath assumes a holiday motif. Then, when a row of full-size brass bells is placed below the wreath, the message is clear and unmistakable. It's a lesson in transformation by well-chosen details.

Wild rose hips predominate in the color scheme of this all-natural wreath. When eighty-three-year-old wreathmaker Mary Hibbard of Hancock, N.H., learned that a favorite field was going to be mowed down, she hurried to collect as many rose hip berries as she could. Some of them ended up in this wreath.

The gentle motion of the wreath comes from angling the spindly plants in the same direction. Eight plants are included in this wreath, which may be surprising because of the careful spacing and shading of color and the expert blending of texture. To a base of Spanish moss, other plants are secured—rose hip fruits, silver king artemisia, white baby's breath, white German statice, wild oregano, the light-green lady's-mantle, and love-in-a-mist pods.

Dried-flower wreaths can have an unsuspecting freshness about them that's especially appealing during the deep winter holidays, and this is one of them. It's a welcome notice that fresh-growing flower blossoms are only a few months away, but in the meantime, let's enjoy these reminders.

This wreath is built on mostly German statice stuck into a straw base. Heather, the pink Rhodanthe, two colors of statice, and love-in-a-mist pods all give this wreath a spirited, blossoming appearance.

This wreath has a more Christmasy tone to it than the previous example, partly because of the red roses, spruce cones, and touches of green. Yet it still is a dried-flower wreath in the fullest sense. Again, a straw base is used to attach German statice, white delphiniums, roses, cones, lamb's ear, and dusty miller. You can dry all these plants yourself by following the directions at the beginning of this section.

In a way, this wreath could pass as a year-round wreath for all of its handsomeness. Its loose but well-considered, well-proportioned construction shows how far a fine sense of aesthetics takes a wreath.

Here's an example of a wreath with a background border to highlight the pink and yellow hues of the flowers. Notice how the border barely shows, but if you remove it, the wreath would lose its special color-enhancing framework. The colors integrate so exquisitely that they almost glow.

The base is a green Styrofoam circle into which the stems are stuck and secured— German statice, baby's breath, straw flowers, the furry bunny's tail, and yellow silk roses. The pink satiny border material is bunched slightly and held to the base by white stickpins. A loop of florist wire is attached to the Styrofoam to hook the wreath on a door or wall.

This wreath is full of action, almost like a Van Gogh whirling sun. What is especially adept of the wreathmaker in this example is the use of color in conjunction with the rotation of the wreath. Instead of the yellows and greens completing the circle, the wreathmaker left the right half blank. This knowing trick-of-the-trade banks on the gestalt of the viewer's imagination to fill in mentally the blank space. This filling-in by the imagination leads to the movement of the wreath. It's a clever design that uses tree ornaments to instill a Noel greeting.

This wreath is replete with symbolism in the German-Austrian tradition. Gertrude Theriault of Austrian Christmas Tree in Manchester, N.H., follows the custom that originated in the Alps in the eighteenth century. Women then gathered together in winter (they were too busy in summer) and made similar wreaths.

The wreaths began as wedding bouquets. They included sugar and spices to symbolize food and blessings for the future. Small mirrors signified protection of the home against evil spirits.

The array of ingredients was intended to display an array of good wishes. For instance, the spices in the wreath represented good health; pearls and gold, prosperity; nuts and kernels, abundance in harvest for the coming year.

Following this tradition, this wreath contains cinnamon sticks, cloves, anise stars, poppy seeds, gingerroot, sugar blocks, peppercorns, caraway and mustard seeds, noodles, nutmeg, acorn pods, cones, beechnuts, chestnuts, hazelnuts, walnuts, almonds, white and pink beans, gold and white pearls. The green leaves are ruscus. Everything is wired to a Styrofoam base. It's a wonderful example of combining symbols of the centuries.

This, too, is made with an Austrian touch. Eighty imported poppy pods are individually wired to a Styrofoam base. Then natural and dyed wild grasses, plus dried and silk flowers, are added. Gold paint glistens from some of the pods. It takes ten hours to make this wreath.

Notice how the interplay of reds and whites keeps the wreath full of detail. At the same time, the spacing and variety of size and shape of the reds and whites remain slightly asymmetrical, never exactly balanced around the circle. The exquisite top hat of red silk poinsettia leaves is all the "ribbon" that's needed.

Cornhusks overlapped and pinned to a straw mold create a Southwestern-type wreath that's singular for its color and texture. You can find cornhusks at some craft shops as well as in some specialty departments of food markets. Trim the husks to a uniform size and angle them in the same direction as you proceed around the wreath base. The choice of decoration is open-ended for this type of wreath, but because of the neutral tone of the husks, bright colors are better. This wreathmaker used shiny red swamp maple berries to perk up the beige husks, along with intriguing lotus pods and baby's breath.

Wreaths make attractive centerpieces. In fact, you can leave them on any table throughout the holiday season. If you make one with candles, as this example, it's perfect for a dining room table—especially for a big family feast.

This wreath is built on a green Styrofoam ring mold. Cranberries are stuck individually on one end of a toothpick, and then the other end is stuck into the mold. Notice how the cranberries are stuck at different heights. This gives an airy depth to the wreath, making it more interesting and less reliant on perfect placement of each cranberry. Notice, too, how the wreathmaker is easy-handed with the white pine needles and dots of baby's breath blossoms, using only enough for a fringe and artful coloring. Metal candle holders can be placed into the mold and then candle adhesive, called Stick-um, placed in the holders to support the candles.

This imaginative wreath is a good example of what to do with a leftover—corks! Mary Ann Lopkato of the North End in Boston saved the corks after she and her husband finished each wine bottle. The corks are glued onto a Styrofoam base and then a Christmas plaid ribbon is tucked between the rows to hide the base and add some color. Of course, an accompanying bunch of artificial grapes makes the fruit symbol, and of course, the signature cork dangling by the bow is the top-ranked cork of all—champagne!

10

Door Decorations

ALTHOUGH wreaths combine an ancient symbolism with an inherent beauty, they are far from the only door decorations. Swags, garlands, potpourri, flower and fruit arrangements, and sprays all can cheer up your door for winter.

Actually, with imagination and good taste, anything goes. Red-felt Santa Clauses with raw white cotton for beard and head signal the season. Antique wooden stocking stretchers enhanced with long flowing ribbon and small cones are sure to provoke curiosity and questions. Decorative brass hunting horns herald in the holidays as no other door decoration can.

The one illustrated opposite shows what a handsome display can be created with only four items—a holiday horn, pink ribbon, silver artemisia, and silk tea roses. The proportions are artful. The bold length of pink, satin-finished, outdoor ribbon announces the unmistakable gaiety of the season; the double bow knot underscores the message with plenty of flair. The tiny tea roses are glued onto the artemisia and enliven the plant with dots of color, suggesting the lightness of small ornaments. Just a few of the roses are added with circumspection to offset the bravado of the rest of the display. All this is assembled with keen thought to the husky brawn of the front door, to make use of the background by choosing the bright pink, the silverness of the artemisia, and the sparkle of the red roses. **107**

This spray is all the more impressive for showing how much drama can be displayed with only three ingredients—red and white silk flowers and evergreen branches. It's a visual lesson in careful assembly. The branches are arranged in an explosion of greenery, thick and dark at the center, thin and translucent at the edge. The strong, mesmerizing starburst effect comes from forming an irregular fringe with some branches extending beyond others. A completely uniform circumference was deliberately avoided to increase the strength of burstlike movement. An odd number of red and white flowers was included to give the decorative part a similar sense of unevenness. The arrangement of the flowers is positioned on a diagonal line to correspond to the major diagonal of the evergreens.

Full-door decorations can be lots of fun and an exuberant welcome for guests. This red door is a perfect place to start. A redecorated fruit basket sliced in half can be filled not only with plants and tree ornaments, as in this example, but also with brightly wrapped gift boxes, toys, or fresh fruits. Take a hint from this one, too, on using French Noel *when the English* Christmas *won't fit your door.*

Long-lost items from your attic might have just the rare shape you need for building a door decoration. This antique stocking stretcher, for example, now serves a function other than collecting dust. One of its new duties is raising questions about what it is in the first place. Some good imagination plus a few laurel branches, berries, and a model partridge-like bird transform both the stocking stretcher and the door. Look around your attic.

This lemon Christmas tree is built on a plywood base with protruding nails to hold the fruit. The laurel leaves are glued to the board for a refreshing, cordial door greeting during the holidays. At this point, the lemons and leaves could be enough, but the inspiring finishing touch of the strings of party ribbon sends you inside with an extra message of gaiety and merrymaking.

Here's another example of the imaginative use of objects for other purposes. For sure, a snowshoe carries its own inherent story of winter. When it's decorated with greens and reds, bright baubles, and shiny ribbons, then a snowshoe sends an oblique, beguiling, witty message for all to enjoy the Christmas season.

117

Supplies

Some wreath bases can be made entirely with materials at home, such as metal coat hangers or cardboard. Other bases, as crimped rings, double-ring molds, Styrofoam rings, can be purchased at craft and hobby stores.

Florist shops usually carry coated spool wire, tape, and greening pins.

Some textile stores and sewing departments stock cloth with Christmas-related designs, such as wreaths, decorated trees, Santa Claus, and candy cane prints.

Tools to make wreaths (scissors and wire cutters) are standard household items found in any hardware or discount store. Electric glue guns may be purchased at craft stores.

The telephone Yellow Pages include information on supplies. Look under "Artificial Flowers," "Artists' Materials and Supplies," "Craft Supplies," "Wreaths," depending on your locale.

Index